T0166844

Bragr

for Suzanne, again

Bragr

Ross Cogan

Seren is the book imprint of
Poetry Wales Press Ltd.
57 Nolton Street, Bridgend, Wales, CF31 3AE
www.serenbooks.com
facebook.com/SerenBooks
twitter@SerenBooks

The right of Ross Cogan to be identified as
the author of this work has been asserted in accordance
with the Copyright, Designs and Patents Act, 1988

© Ross Cogan, 2018

ISBN: 978-1-78172-455-2
ebook: 978-1-78172-453-8
Kindle: 978-1-78172-454-5

A CIP record for this title is available from the British Library.

All rights reserved. No part of this publication may be reproduced,
stored in a retrieval system, or transmitted at any time or by any means,
electronic, mechanical, photocopying, recording or otherwise without
the prior permission of the copyright holder.

The publisher acknowledges the financial assistance of the Welsh Books Council.

Cover artwork: © Jamie Hill at Seren.

Author photograph: © John Cogan

Printed in Bembo by Bell & Bain Ltd, Scotland.

Contents

Part I – The beginning

The beginning	9
Time thaws	11
Ymir's skull	12
Ash	13
Beech	14
Willow	15
The grain	16
Idun	17
Attraction	18
In your hands	19
Field pattern	20
Lapstrake	21
And the rest	22
Traefisk	23
The fish sing like birds	24
Aurvandil's toe	25
Loki as falcon	26

Part II – Bestiary

Bees swarming	29
Calf	30
Chicken	31
Ducks	32
Goats	33
Hare	34
Lizards	35
Moths	36
Otter	37
Pheasant	38
Pigeon	39
Rat	40
Ravens	41
Seagull	42
Snakes	43
Swan	45
Toad	46

Part III – Ragnarök

Loki as salmon	49
Kvasir's blood	50
Poem / Prayer	51
Lord of the gallows	52
Plague metal	53
Baldr's dreams	54
Fenrir bound	55
The sea gives up its dead	56
The wolves eat the sun	57
Ragnarök	58
Wreath	60
Notes	61
Acknowledgements	63

Part I

The beginning

The beginning

1.
Onething was the first. That is all we know
of Onething. Some say you could not see
Onething as you could not stand outside it,
as Onething was everything. Some say it wore
no sheen; that it would swallow the light.
But there was no light. Some say 'I know
what went before Onething'. They lie. There was
no-thing before Onething, not even 'before'.
Nor even 'after'. So, when I say 'then
Onething split like an egg' I also lie.

2.
And yet it split, quartered like a traitor
and there were four things. The first froze,
retreating like a beaten army behind
the ramparts of matter, where it crouches
clothed in a coat of fizzing flesh.
This is defence, strength and silence,
unity and endurance.

3.
The next thing slipped between close things
like the water round the shoal, the mortar in the wall.
It brings with it alliance, friendship and family,
sex and loyalty.
Through it things meet, bond and grow.

4.
The third thing flooded
the great gaps between far things.
Stretched like a taut net it touches
all things at once, not minding time.
This signifies speed, freedom and flight,
language and travel.

5.
The last thing, like
the first, fled to the hot heart
of flesh, but as spy not warden,
the wasp in the fruit. We call this 'weak'
but it is the weakness that achieves by yielding.
Like water working on a joint it drives
wedges into fine faults, slyly splitting
and shifting things, levelling and building.
It is the force of difference, of chaos and change,
chance and creation. Through it all things
entered the world: sea and sky;
sun and stars; planets and poetry;
tragedy and magic; gold and good;
trees, heat, seasons, helium and evil.
Also Ymir, first of the frost giants,
whose leg incestuously sired a son
on his other leg – an auspicious start
for the gaudy carnival of Gods and men.

6.
Don't think though that Onething is lost or gone.
The uncarved block, it abides blindly
in the teeming creatures, and in the great spaces
eyelessly watching, mindlessly waiting.
Men talk of love, but men know nothing.
This is just stark force feeling its strength,
beating the bounds of the nine worlds,
drawing itself up, waiting for the crunch.

Time thaws

Fire and ice. Before time thawed
and thread-like cracks cleaved through weeks,
sent days drifting, snapping off hours,
sowing a spray, a foam of moments,
like a stream stirring, shedding its skin
of snow-dusted ice, there were two worlds
waiting. Muspell; fire-world. Baking
black soil steamed, hissed in the heat;
hardened like that crust baked round the rim
of the stew bowl. And Black Surt sat
and still sits, safe in his rock-like hide
a stone monk, one bloody eye
scanning the sky from beneath his skin
for the sign to light the last pyre,
the blue touch paper for the big crunch.
Niflheim; ice-world. Sunless and brittle,
laid out like glass around the impossibly
gargling Hvergelmir, roaring kettle
that rises at Helgrind, sloughs off sons
– sluggish streams that pick up pack ice
like parasites, until they stumble
and freeze in furrows. Fire and ice.
End and end. One world burns,
crumbles, slumps wheezing inward
as the space is squeezed from each atom.
One world freezes, dies in the dark,
slowly as a seaman swept from the deck
his limbs numbed as his lungs fill up.
Fire and ice. And something else.
Can you hear a tick, ticking,
an urgent tap, water on stone?

Ymir's skull

Scraped clean of its skin, the ice-white skull
of Ymir, first and greatest of the frost giants,
still rinsed in a thin wash of sunset blood,
was shoved and shouldered like blue stone and sarsen;
rigged over the earth like a bone awning.

This brain-hall filled quickly with bright guests;
the go-cart sun; the hospital-trolley moon
wheeled through on its cast-iron casters;
planets like wandering lute players;
shoals of stars swimming in circles.

Some, the sources note, evolved to live
further from earth in the thinnest air.
Polaris, the North Star, say the sagas
is furthest of all, as it moves least –
a piece of false but plausible logic

held like a hand towel over this tall tale
to lend it some shreds of specious sense
perhaps. Or perhaps to counterpoint the truth
that we are as ephemeral as thoughts
bubbling and bursting under a bone sky.

Ash

From a drowned tree spread-eagled on the beach
Odin carved a man. First he cured
the drenched wood, stacking the log
with others where the wind could feel round it
like a poacher tickling a trout. Then he took
the log and laid it safely on his saw bench,
stripped its bark, planed and sanded
it smooth, set to work with a sharp chisel.
Like all creators he could see the shape shimmer
under the surface; alternative forms
of eyes and hands jostling on the pages
of the painter's notebook. He stroked the grain,
dipped the tip of the chisel in like a baited
hook and dredged up knotted limbs,
hands and head, the dense log melting
to flesh under his kneading palms.
Ash it was. Straight, dark, silvery wood,
the same as flourishing, suffering Yggdrasil,
the wounded world-tree; the favourite wood
for spades and scythes, for straight-flying spears.

Beech

Coming home at dusk and the air behind
the bare beech tree is pressing out some late
light through querns of cloud. The sky is lined
with sedimentary varves: dark veins of slate
capping scarlet sandstones; layers of shale
settling in muddy sheets; and here and there
a seam of denim blueschist or a stale
loaf of crumbling limestone pointing to where

the sun has gone. The bare limbs of the beech
explore the sky's pillowed geology,
tenderly sift the different strata, reach
between the seams like roots, as if a tree
could turn the earth, rotate the world around,
reveal a new world blooming underground.

Willow

Planted in the soil, like Joseph's staff,
the willow branch we'd used to mark a row
of cauliflowers tucked in beside the path
came back to life, budded, started to grow,
put on a shoal of slender, silver-green,
fish-shaped leaves strung like bunches of keys,
and so began to ink itself between
the corrugated trunks of older trees.

It stood three years before we tore it down.
By then its leaves were dense; as it reached higher
its shadow spread. Its roots had also grown,
sucked moisture from the soil. We built a fire,
burned it, not saving some for kindling even.
We rarely want the miracles we're given.

The grain

The sharp-tongued plane like a glacier strips
the topsoil from a plank. And there it is
exposed: the grain. A contour map of peaks

and plains, valleys tugging bell-ropes of streams,
straight-sided cliffs; the wooden veins in short
crushed to an atlas plate. And as the sheets

of leaf-thin parings roll from the blade's press
they form a frame of scrolls around the piece
of thinning wood as if to mark its loss.

Idun

Brown-eyed Idun, with her leaf-green scarf
bound round her white flesh like the smooth wax
of an apple, balances a fruit basket –
puzzle of moss-packed rush and willow –
in her arm's bow, so that it strokes her hip.

The sweet, gold-skinned fruit hold a white-
coated claim: that they will tame time,
dam up minutes, redirect ruffling days
down other courses, leaving us dry
like islands. But I know that the real sorcery

is in the angle of shoulder and hip, tangle
of plaited hands like a detail in stone
from a tomb sculpture; the smiling grace
that gives love with an apple – the only thing
truly immortal in all the gimcrack heavens.

Attraction

In bed you bring your knees up to my thigh;
hand to my chest, you let your fingers trail
in hair like waterweed. And there you lie:
the U-shaped magnet to my iron nail.

In your hands

I wonder at the small bones that you keep
locked in your hands' chapel, tight in their sleeves

of skin like the white chalk under downland.
And I wonder at the way they mesh, side laid

on side, tips touching like a clinker keel,
or fall open showing boundary, canal.

Lend me your palms' heat; let me reorder
their small muscles, tangle my own fingers

in yours, neat as the beams beneath the slate.
Cast your dice for me. Show me my fate.

Field pattern

Eventually the soil will invade.
Digging has rubbed the fingers where I hold

the spade, thinning the skin, leaving the thread-
veins bare like the sedge-grass roots at low tide

or the wiring in a cheap room. And soon
the topsoil burrows in, etching a brown

tattoo into the flesh, as a slow stream
drops silt into the body of a farm.

The side of my finger now wears a field
pattern: a tangle of dark borders around

pastures of skin like a tithe map to show
the dust staking a title to its own.

Lapstrake

Here you can walk across mudstone and mud
flat, through sedge into a river grown
fat as now, forgetting the tithe of land
taxed from its banks, it ponders borders with
the fierce sea and braids itself to brown
dreadlocks of estuary. Shadowed beneath

an ankle of low cliff is a flat spit
of shale and shingle lent to the windless reach.
Here we can launch. Haul the complaining boat,
breastbone scraping on stone, into the bay;
revive it in water, let its sails catch
the push of air and, filling, pull away.

'Sea kind' the old men call it. With the staves
rolled round their slotted bones then folded in
so side overlies side, they mimic waves'
own lines of rush and fall – at least they do
as well as our loose mapping ever can –
and grip the stream firm as a well-soled shoe

holds snow. The craft that is lapstrake made
turns live to the tiller but still forgives
a clumsy touch. It rests poised as a hand
held palm upwards upon a river's glass
table or treads in diced sea, light as a leaf.
Watch it well. This is the best of us.

And the rest

The poem wounds the page.
The painting marks the plain

wall with a bruise. The keys
rattle like loose teeth

in the piano's face.
The fiddle scratches its name

onto the wind; the stone
is unwillingly clothed;

the dancer drops. Direct,
then, your senses instead

to the sudden clearing
that only appears

after the last, busy
note has finished hissing;

the point an inch below
the final line of the poem

where the page is still bright
and trackless. Just there. See it?

Traefisk

I hooked my chisel-tip into the pine
wood block, played it with tenon saw and plane

until its shape grew clear like a brown trout
rising from weeds. Then on a steel point

I landed it. I gave it socket eyes,
wrapped it in half-moon armour, scored the fine

folds of its tail. But you, you made it bloom,
coloured its sides in silvers, greens and blues,

clothed it in silk ribbons and placed it high
up in the knotted cradle of a tree

where the light could find it, where it might
just be confused with something that can fly.

The fish sing like birds

Sometimes, at night, when the dog wind
has done herding the water round

we rise and point our polished tea-
spoon faces at the moon, slowly

circling – a drowned canteen stirring
the sea. And as we carve our curves

on the night's crust with our nib tails
we start to shed our scales; they fall

like showers of notes through a dark space.
And in their place thickets of waving

feathers – maybe they're gills or fronds –
carpet us in yellows and reds

and blues. Then we unglue our lips,
lift our eyes, our pillowy mouths up

over the lid, and though not built
for things like this, though we are out

of our element, though we lack
a larynx even, yet we hold back

our heads and in our tinkling, tin-
foil voices open our throats and sing.

Aurvandil's toe

If we could but see it, the night
would be fat with stars. Not only the gaudy
plume of Polaris, spatter of constellations,
but tiny translucent fragments of candles.
If we had millwheel eyes the sky
would not be sown with stars like the seeded field,
the flock in flight, gold on the dark cloak;
it would squirm with bright lights like the grain
hopper, the nest of naked grubs,
sand settling on the borderless shore.
The night would blind us with its unnumbered suns.

But then if we could really see depth
with fulcrum eyes rolling the universe,
or like Gods could fold space in time's amber
our gaze would freeze in the lean gaps
between the fires. And so, knowing this
somehow, we hang the dark with our clutter:
belts and bears, horses and ploughs
fishes and rams and bows and best
of all, the toe of Aurvandil the Brave,
which, poking from Thor's knapsack, grew black
with frostbite and snapped, and was hurled by the God
into orbit. A frostbitten toe set on high;
the last, best charm against the dark.

Loki as falcon

I slide the skin on over my own skin;
cold, corpse-like it is and cratered where quills
stand in their inkwells. A savage eye
I shrug on too and a barrage of sharp moons.
My new flesh knows the call of a thermal,
the joyful song of the ploughed field I can ride

real as a stream while this raiment of sails
sets and trims itself again and again
with each new note. Caves have been cut
in my bones; my shriek splits clouds like the shrill
scrape of iron on whetstone. When I return
youth lies in my talons, tight as a nut.

Part II

Bestiary

Bees swarming

No, not a dance. This is older,
cruder, moved by the same power

that fires planets in a star's kiln.
A galaxy is being spun

between the pear tree and the wall.
Polished amber suns purl and wheel;

those furthest out in lazy arcs
like circling gulls; nearer the dark

axis a writhing crowd. This is
the whirlwind that conceals Zeus;

it is the double helix, the smoke
unravelled from the altar-blackened

offering, and that murmur the hum
of voices calling from another room.

Calf

As we change backdrops in the album's toy
theatre, its card arches give on to posed
domestic scenes: a sailor-suited boy
clutching his yacht; the family enclosed
in three decorous walls; the wedded pair –
mutton-chop whiskered, leg-of-mutton sleeved.
And then a shock. Finding the body where
it died, fearing he wouldn't be believed

perhaps, one of these bull-faced farmers took
it back through April puddles, posed each head
with care, pasted the image in his book
to gaze out with its four glazed eyes, its dead,
swelling twin tongues. That's how history speaks
to us: through doomed monsters and gentle freaks.

Chicken

After I had taken off his head
with my hatchet I hung him by his feet
on an ash tree so that the blood drained out.
Then feeling through the feathers for the dead
flesh of his thighs, stretching it tight, I tore
layers of fine white down from off his breast,
his legs, his tail and back. I left to last
the crisp blades on his wings, burrowed secure

in their foxholes. Peter pinned to the cross,
heels-over-head, naked, his cooling skin,
his breast bruised to the flush of ruby wine,
his spear-struck side. Blood pooled bright on the grass
and his blind corpse fell back to earth even
as his arms were decked with the favours of heaven.

Ducks

I
Triangle of ducks
sits in the table's ripe shade
like three white Buddhas.

II
Beaks slipped under wings
each one keeps an eye open:
coal on trackless snow.

III
The ducks' eyes are green.
So how are they also wine-
dark as Homer's sea?

IV
The song of ducks is
opening hinges and small
machines starting up.

V
Like thieves the ducks reach
through the water's lid and bring
out diamond chaplets.

Goats

The goats talk by fighting, their words
spun by rotors into codes

of scrapes and blows. Angle of ear,
of spine and tail is their grammar

while horns white as fossils display
a simple scratched language, like clay

seals or tally sticks. The goats
lounge lop-sided in the heat,

awnings of hip rigged over the ribbed
vaults of their torsos; ears tilted

down; eyes shrunk to oblongs; jaws
milling tangled fibres of bruised

grass and browse. The goats are. New
kingdoms take shape in their marrow.

Hare

Watched from the window of a moving train –
near where the rail embankment slid away
to free, unshaven scrub, then rose again
to make a sort of ring, walled with a spray
of willow-herb and birch – my first real hare.
A ragged batch of old man's clothes on bent
hangers, a high-strung eye; it smelt the air
for death, sieving its well-stocked streams for scent

of fox or dog, then kicked its rebec legs,
leant into the wind and went. My first real hare.
Sometimes – rarely – some weird thing unpegs
our playhouse scenery. Watching it there
through the smeared glass was like glimpsing my face
in the gold pages of a book of days.

Lizards

"Truth is like a lizard; it leaves its tail in your fingers and runs away knowing perfectly well that it will grow a new one in a moment."
— Ivan Turgenev

It's as they leave we see them, whip-thin tail
taking the morning's pulse, translating it
to cosine curves of spine; the two back feet
reading danger in the dust and soil,

tasting the Braille of leaf mould. Only once
I drew curtains of fern and on a stone
like bronze, worked on an anvil head, a clan
settled in green ranges under the sun.

I clutched at them. Then I think I recall
the startled joy at seeing myth made real
in severed flesh, flash of green feet, a tail
tip, pinched in thumb and finger, starting to cool.

Moths

Not the big ones, not
the Underwings, the Hawks,
Emperors, Tigers,
the Death's Heads, the Silver
Ys. Not the ones that
unclasp their black hinges
and clack into the lights:
motes perhaps by day
on a wall's white face.

Rather the Cabbages,
the Snouts, the Clouded Drabs,
the Quakers: those that rise
like steam as your feet crush grass.
Grey-veined seed parcels,
their stumbling flight unseen,
they pass hours in your houses.
You sweep their unrigged husks
from your window sills.

Otter

Its old-man-monkey hands worked on a cake
of salmon, solving riddles of oil and scent,
unpicking knots of flesh, carving a point
with cunning teeth. I saw once, on the bank,

watching me with the slow eyes of an earl
a big dog otter, his pelt beaten red-gold
in the early evening's embers. And as I stood
barely breathing, he rose, uncurled his tail

then slung the full bag of his body on
the stream's shoulders and let the water pull
it away 'til just a bobbing dot of skull
was left; a skull that might have been human.

Pheasant

The hen was struck as she landed, pulled down
the tunnel under the truck, where the exhaust
and axles caught and tore her, and she burst
beneath the twin back wheels. But while her brown
tussock of corpse falls on the road, a spray
of feathers like a gasp of blackened snow
lifts in the lorry's wake, pauses, then blows
across my misted windscreen and away.

I thought then of those painters who drew the soul,
leaving the dying body, as a dove
flying above the deathbed on its ascent
to heaven, and glancing backwards – to console
perhaps, or with relief? And so we drove
on through the slipstream of a sacrament.

Pigeon

Pushed from its nest early, the air not thick
enough beneath its unripe wings, it fell
and died under the lime. I found the chick
face upwards like a toppled finial,
its stubby wing buds splayed heraldically;
a pea-sized brooch of blood dried on its cheek.
Without its adult feathers I could see
its lizard skin, the granite of its beak

an undergrowth of quills, and a cold eye
battened beneath the silo of its lid,
blank and terrible. When we untie
fossils from the layers of shale amid
which they've waited like phrases in a book
that's what they show: those granite lines; that look.

Rat

For weeks we left each other signs, like spies:
a foot-rune stylused on a patch of clay;
bullet-shaped droppings stacked up like supplies;
a tape of tail spooling its getaway.
And I replied in alphabets of death,
making curt lines of traps that spoke through rows
of steel teeth and leaving them beneath
the bushes where I thought I'd seen it go.

It never triggered one. It never ate
the poison I put down. For weeks I saw
no signs, until I found it by the gate
in the long grass, eyeless and with a raw
tear in its fur from which the bright guts spilt
like the map of a city no one ever built.

Ravens

Black thought, with its soap–bubble plumage,
its tight, jewelled eye, its damage of talons,
flies faster than falcons, visits past
and future. Black memory, a battered purse,
preens irritably. The past is its place
drilling the middens with its alloy bill.
Allfather's subtle spies, he sends them after
the white bones of the hanged and butchered;
also the state secret, the senate scandal,
the sex shame of the soap starlet,
the lost laptop and the unguarded letter.
They talk to him in their parchment voices
and he dreams chaos. But I also have agents.
At daybreak they watch him release the ravens,
see as they shrink to twin pupils
beneath a cloud's brow. They know his biggest
fear: that someday he will send them out
a last time, and lost, they won't return.
And he will not know that they are lost.

Seagull

The gulls' language is oil
and small, dead things in pools.

The words lurch from their throats
like something wet prized-out

of a shell, something old
with no place in the world.

The gulls have songs as well.
They're delicate and formal

as gill flaps bleached to book-
yellow and stripped-down like

turbines or bones leaning,
leering out of their sleeves.

Seagulls have fifty-four
different words for anger.

Snakes

(I)

All beauty hauls a freight of fear
melded as tin in bronze. When I saw

it scrawled onto my border like
a grade or a proof-reader's mark

I knew that it was dead. But still
that human it-will-bite-your-heel

instinct sat up in me and I flinched,
spade gripped ready to strike-its-head.

And yet it was gorgeous. As straight
as an auger, its light, jade scales

might have been combed butter, but would
steer it, I knew, through the hill's side.

Gently I raised it like a sleeping
child, a lover, a green-skinned apple.

(II)

Lifting the large planter, there was
a Gorgon's head of tiny snakes.

For a moment they lay frozen
as if made marble by their own

cool gaze. And then calmly, with the nod
of young nobles, they sought the shade

again. Princes do not rush; their
flight was a yawn, a wave. Fingers

and thumb slipping from a loosened fist.
Loop slid over loop as if

they could hunt time through the piled hay;
catch it sure as they caught their tails.

Swan

Shortly after she died they washed her slight
body and sewed it into hides with sweet,
clean-scented herbs and petals, as you might
keep clothes from moths. Later they dug a neat,
narrow shaft, lined it with stone and laid
a single swan's wing in the grave to cover
the ground under her corpse, before the spade
turned back the soil and scraped the dark loam over.

And when we dug her up the flesh and hide
had gone, but the quills had stamped a barcode in
the soil. And the child's bones, and the wing beside
which they'd lain for centuries like a twin,
had jostled together in the loam and might
have been some new thing that aspired to flight.

Toad

The toad is a dropped glove sucking
on a shoelace of air. Its sack

of loose skin, mottled under leaves,
heaves damply with the strain of breathing

this thin sky. Only with the dark
does it tread the borders – its walk

a slow, repeated falling checked
on the hinge; a stone on sapling legs.

The toad opens its emerald eye,
lets in the teeming world; tonight

in the shallow pools that the rain
has sown, it will consume the moon.

Part III

Ragnarök

Loki as salmon

Leaf-shaped scales like shield-walls slide
smoothly, row over row. My arms,
shrunk to bony tongues, have sprouted
silk sails between dipstick fingers.
Fused knees hinge sideways now, slapping
me fast upstream, or wheeling like rotors
as the water feels around me. Plate mail flanked,
my bowl-eyes brim with the green light that drips
from trees. I am the trickster, the great shape-shifter
shrugging skins on and off, like scowls and smiles.
It was for me that they invented nets.

Kvasir's blood

In the gloom of the backroom, Galar and Fjalar
sprung the trap like pros. Each had stowed
a stiletto up his sleeve, and as Kvasir shuffled
into the shade they struck, front and back,
the sharp steel synchronised, spitting
him like souvlaki. Kvasir sighed, slumped,
the wind leaving him like a leaking lilo.

The two killers propped the corpse up in a corner,
pressed bowls to the wounds' red lips, and drained
the viscous, spit-like blood; by the time
the body was a wrinkled, white wineskin
they had filled two vats, Son and Bodn.
Then they added herbs to stop it clotting
and brewed it with honey to make a fine mead.

Kvasir's blood is also called Son's Store,
Ship of the Dwarves and Suttung's Mead,
but mostly the Mead of Poetry. The few
allowed to drink gain skill in song
and all the use of words; it's a sweet brew
but strong – each real poem bears the print
of a God's lips outlined in blood.

Poem / Prayer

And so we dragged him in to die, swilled-out
the mouths carved into chest and neck, fed them
with herbs; took off his coat, loosened his shirt,

removed his shoes. We didn't ask his name
for that would be unsafe and we had risked
enough already. But we did search him

for papers. And we found some sort of list
we couldn't read, a thin wallet, a small
packet of something sweet. He wouldn't rest,

kept hinging his trunk, raising his lips, but all
that did was make the viscous ranks of blood
march more quickly, overrunning the bowl

we'd left to hold them in. And then he tried
to speak − a jagged rattle like a nail
in a petrol can. We didn't understand

the battered foreign words, but we could feel
their weight. They had been picked and dressed with care
and went about their work in a calm, well-

drilled way like a burial detail. There
was the hint of incense in them and the drum
of waves. 'Was it a poem or a prayer?'

I thought. The ragged slits let into skin
wept red; his chapped lips worked over their list.
And I thought 'Was it a prayer or a poem?'

Lord of the gallows

To learn writing I spent nine days dead,
hung by my heels, stabbed in the side
with an ash spear, while ravens ripped
my greening flesh, my one good eye.
At first I owned only the one word,
let it riot like a child round my head's hall,
kicking out its kid-like-letter legs.
I learn, though, that words soon spread
like the threads of space that root through sheet ice
cracking it into ragged zones of control.

As I nurtured my new knowledge, I found words
to ease grief and to heal heart-woe;
charms to cure illness or prolong pain.
I can disarm a huge host at a distance,
turn another's bile so it rebounds, burning.
I listen to the dead and speak to the unborn.

But the words in turn have settled my skull
like dreams or the weevils in the grain silo,
or the small molecules that slip through the membrane,
or the plague rats that run through the port.
They build their barracks and their memorials,
reason's straight streets and fiction's mazes.
It's right that I am called the one-eyed:
I see everything clearly and I am blind.

Plague metal

Snake metal, writhing in the forge light
scale over scale like bright water
served to a low sun. If a sword
could be water, encircling the slow shield,
eroding it, breaching your armour, reaching
into your skin like a taproot seducing
the soil, this would be it. If plague
could be drawn into lines, carded like wool,
woven into shining death and worn,
this would be it. It is sex compressed
to a dense point, reeling in eyes
on taut, bright threads. It is power,
the right of kings to rule beaten
to a badge, clipped to a cloak. Freyja,
whose tears are gold, was so dazzled
by the Brisingamen she let her limbs
be mortgaged, laid back, spread her legs
for the four hideous smiths. Loki
stole the brooch for Odin; to save
his hide became a flea and hid
in Freyja's bed, bit her neck.
And Odin, chaos lover, cheerleader
for death, who longed to set emperors,
with their kings and minor kings, at odds,
watch their war bands spill over landscapes
hacking limbs, heaving their iron
axeheads into skulls' brittle baskets,
sinking spears in the moist maze of guts,
what did he do? What do you think?

Baldr's dreams

Night, and skull-guests like slugs
seep from the topsoil of ploughed sleep;
squirming stomachs on a slime-stream,
wide mouths in their white, eyeless chests.
Deliberate as florid Tory clubmen
they graze on my brain's rich plot;
each day I wake lessened on sweat-
soaked sheets.
            Odin cast the runes
over me. Then they tried me on Prozac,
Zoloft, Luvox, Lexapro and Paxil;
infusions of Purslane and St John's Wort;
the talking cure; shocks; bones; silence.
Finally, Allfather saddled Sleipnir,
his eight-legged horse born of Loki,
and turned his nose north to Niflheim,
past Garm the guard dog and into Hel's hall
where the vague dead envy the quick.
There Odin the wise spoke with a seeress,
asked her the meaning of my nightmares,
was told that they foreshadow my death
at the hands of Hod my blind half-brother,
that the clock was counting down to Ragnarök.

The dreams remain. Only now they're welcome.
My kind skull-guests are a soul-fasting.
Like leeches on a greening wound, they want
just to prune me, to smooth my steps,
so when at last the friendly dart
is thrown, it can pass harmless through me.

Fenrir bound

Von, the spit-stream, slides into Amsvartnir
the black, fishless lake. It froths
round molar-stones, polished cobbles,
paving Fenrir's toad-hide tongue.
Loki's son lies under Lyngvi, his jaws
tacked shut with Tyr's sword.
Surrounding him are stacked the split links
of a great, fat chain, like sawn logs.
His sleeping-puppy's feet twitch
in the slender knots of Gleipnir – the thin
silk thread forged by the dark smiths,
they said, from impossible things: the breath
of fish; the sound of stalking cats;
a mountain's roots. Dumb Fenrir bound
himself, surely, fooled by the smiths' nonsense.

Perhaps. Or perhaps he read the fates' expressions,
decided to rest, wait for Ragnarök
snug as a siloed Titan warhead.
He is Loki's son; he knows that Gods
also need to believe.
                        Fenrir's huge head
stirs sometimes, shaking cities of lice;
a caked eye rolls; he tastes again the gore
of Tyr's right hand quickening his spit.
His feet tick on like a countdown.

The sea gives up its dead

When it returned them they were changed;
so much so that we could only tell
one from another by the small, sacred things
they wore:
the lockets sheltering their locks of hair;
the tangled silver rings;
the spine-cracked book bent back and plunged
still open in the well
of a coat. It was too late to take them then from where
the sea had laid them on the shore;

the small ranks of keen teeth
bred in the sea's belly had cut
and torn laces of flesh from their faces and hands
until the bones
peered through. And the sea itself had mauled
them, turned them on its lathe of stones,
planed ears and nose as the turner smooths a knot
and worked its way beneath
the softening, greening skin. The corpses we hauled
with boat hooks up the sand

were not fit for the earth. And since the sea
had returned them we offered them instead
to the sky; built a pyre
under them and watched as the sodden meat
became breath
in the lungs of the fire
while the bones glowed filament red.
And in the dark the sea growled softly –
an old song that was at once a death
rattle and a heartbeat.

The wolves eat the sun

Before the shutdown the wolves will start working
together. Hati who hounds the moon,
Sköll who stalks the sun through the lush sky,
massive Managarm, and Fenrir, freed
at last from Lyngvi, will coordinate forces
in that way wolves do, like muscles in an arm
or the members of a terror cell. As one
they'll trail the moon across the jet road;
baying, bring it down, like a trapped stag;
test their teeth on its bleached bones.
Then, with threads of flesh unfurled in their mouths,
they'll head off after the scurrying sun.

And the flight paths will run
with pearly blood; tons of dust
will blacken the stratosphere. The sibyl says
this: for years after the sun will be dark
the winds vicious, the sea will smash
the land.
          Fear lies at the core of all things.
Look at the moon. Can you not see the skull?

Ragnarök

After Milosz

When it comes, and it will, it will come on
a plain weekday, perhaps in early spring
or autumn, a frowsy day, one that woke late
and got dressed in a hurry without care
quite forgetting
to comb its hair, which anyway got damp

in the almost rain. When it comes the slugs
will have been on the lettuces again,
chiselling their sickle moons; starlings will sit
like notes on a stave while below them men spray
hectares of grain
with a lake of liquid manure. A snake

will riffle its green belt through the fern stems
and the flies will alight on a dead shrew.
When it comes a young woman will be
formatting the numbers in her spreadsheet
as she scrolls through
a list of annual reports. The bond

salesman will have made the biggest trade
of his career; sparrows will jive outside
in the puddles; fungi will start to fling
armfuls of spores into the air; a spent
rabbit will hide
shaking from the hounds. And when it comes

the man in the fourteenth-floor flat, the one
the other tenants never see, will pop
a pill and think again of his dead child.
The women walking in the park behind
their prams will stop
to hear the song unfurl through the window.

The slaughtermen will have stained their gloves red
with slick, bright blood; tectonic plates will move
under the sea a fraction of an inch
and cause no harm; a poet will write sadly
of his lost love
and pick his nose. The President will put

the final touches to the plan for peace.
Don't be surprised then if you fail to spot
the golden ranks of heroes or the massed
brigades of ogres. These days they wear grey
and look a lot
like each other. But they remain heroes

and ogres, and their swords gleam in their bags.
A one-eyed man will pull on his broad-brimmed hat
and stalk away. Please don't expect a warning.
This is a whimper not a bang. But it's
a whimper that
will level hills and drown the suffering world.

Wreath

The limbs I lopped in March from the horse chestnut
and stored bundled upright by the woodshed
had, two months later, bloomed. First the twigs put
on neat turbans, sweet-swelling, sticky red/
brown buds, rutted where fold overlapped fold.
And then, in May, the polished nibs slid back
and spilt slim, green, sinuous stems; unrolled
their empty sacks of leaves, shrivelled for lack

of sap. I'd not expected this, that these
lewd, amputated limbs should still contain
the clean, readable blueprints of their trees
and enough life to put on leaves again;
that this sad, small, withered and wilting wreath
might be a charm against, or cure for, death.

Notes

p.10. *Ymir.* The first of the Jötnar or frost giants, he was formed from venom dripping from the ice rivers, or Élivágar, that flowed in the primordial void. Odin, together with his brother Gods Vili and Vé, later killed him and fashioned the earth from his body.

The uncarved block. An early Daoist metaphor for the natural, simple state of humanity.

p.11. *Muspell... Surt... Niflheim... Hvergelmir... Helgrind.* Muspell or Muspelheim is a realm of fire ruled over by Surt (or Surtr) a fire giant. Together with Niflheim (or Nifheimr) a world of mist and ice, it is one of the two primordial worlds from which the nine worlds of Norse myth emerged. Hvergelmir means 'boiling spring' and all waters are said to rise from it. Helgrind is the main entrance to Hel, the underworld, sometimes conflated with Niflheim.

p.12. *Ymir.* See note p.10.

p.13. *Yggdrasil.* The 'world tree', traditionally an ash, which connects the nine worlds. The name seems to mean 'Odin's Horse' (i.e. gallows) referring to the fact that Odin hung from it to learn writing (see note to p.52). The first people were carved by Odin from two trees found on the seashore; the man was called Ask (Ash) and the woman Embla (Elm).

p.17. *Idun* (or Idunn). The wife of Bragi, God of poetry. She is the keeper of the golden apples that allow the Gods to enjoy eternal youth.

p.21. *Lapstrake.* Another name for clinker built.

p.23. *Traefisk.* In Danish 'wooden fish'.

p.24. *'The fish sing like birds'.* Inspired by a quote from Halldór Laxness, Iceland's only Nobel Laureate: "We have to prove to the rest of the world that the fish can sing just like a bird". From *Meltdown Iceland*, Roger Boyes' book on the Icelandic banking crisis.

p.25. *Aurvandil.* The husband of the sibyl Gróa, he was rescued by Thor from the land of the giants in a basket. The name means 'bright wanderer' and may refer to the morning star.

p.26. *Loki.* Loki is the trickster God, a highly ambiguous figure. Having helped the giant Thiazi (or Thjazi) to abduct Idun and steal her golden apples, he transforms into a falcon to retrieve her from Jötunheim. To do so he changes her into a nut.

p.33. *In their marrow.* Tanngrisnir and Tanngnjóstr ('teeth-barer' and 'teeth-grinder') are the goats that pull Thor's chariot. They can be eaten and then resurrected from their bones and hides. Thjálfi, son of a peasant family with whom Thor stays, breaks one of the leg bones to eat the marrow, leading to the goat being lamed, for which he pays by becoming Thor's servant.

p.37. *Otter.* Ótr (or Ott, Otr, Ottar, Otter) is the son of king (or farmer-magician) Hreidmar and a shape-changer. Odin, Honir and Loki meet him in the form of an otter and kill him, for which they have to pay a weregeld. This involves filling Ótr's pelt with gold and covering it with gold until none of it shows. Loki steals the gold from the dwarf Andvari, who curses it.

61

p.41. *Ravens.* Huginn ('thought') and Muninn ('memory') fly over the world to bring information to Odin. See *Grimnismal* ('Grimnir's Sayings') in *The Poetic Edda.*

Allfather. One of Odin's many names.

p.43. *Straight as an augur.* Having forced the giant Baugi to drill a hole through a mountain with an augur, Odin turns himself into a snake to steal the mead of poetry from Suttung.

p.45. *Swan.* From a real excavation in Denmark, detailed by Steven Mithen in *After the Ice: A Global Human History 20,000 to 5,000 BC.*

p.49. *Salmon.* When the disgraced Loki went on the run from the Gods he spent his days transformed into a salmon. Far-seeing Odin found him, however, and Thor caught him using the first net – a net that Loki had designed to catch fish but had tried to burn.

p.50. *Kvasir… Galar and Fjalar.* Kvasir was a wise being born from the Gods' saliva. He is killed by the dwarfs Galar and Fjalar, who mix his blood with honey to brew the mead of poetry, which gives the drinker wisdom and the power of verse.

p.52. *Lord of the gallows.* Another of Odin's names. Odin spent nine days and nights hanging on a branch of Yggdrasil, wounded in the side with a spear and offered 'to himself', in order to gain knowledge of the runes – both their forms and their uses.

p.53. *Brisingamen.* The necklace of Freyja, the goddess of love, beauty and fertility, but also linked with gold, war and death. It was forged by four dwarfs whose price was that the goddess spent a night with each of them. On Odin's orders Loki stole it, in the process becoming a flea. The condition he set on its return was that Freyja agreed to stir up hatred on earth.

p.54. *Baldr* (also Baldur, Balder). Son of Odin and Frigg and the best loved of the Gods. He grew depressed by a series of dreams foretelling his death, so Frigg made everything on earth vow not to hurt him. She overlooked mistletoe, however, and on learning this Loki made a spear of mistletoe, which he gave to blind Hod (or Hödr) to throw at his brother Baldr.

p.55. *Fenrir.* A giant wolf, the son of Loki with the giantess Angrboda. At Ragnarök Fenrir will kill Odin before being killed by Odin's son Vidarr.

Amsvartnir… Lyngvi… Gleipnir. Lyngvi is the Island in the middle of the lake of Amsvartnir ('pitch black'), where the Gods bound Fenrir with Gleipnir, a slender thread of incredible power forged by dwarfs from impossible things.

Tyr. A God of law and military glory. The only way that Fenrir would consent to being bound was for one of the Gods to put their right hand in his mouth as a mark of good faith.

p.57. *Hati… Sköll… Managarm.* Hati Hródvitnisson ('he who hates'), Sköll ('treachery') and Managarm (or Mánagarmr, 'moon-hound') are wolves. The former two are sons of Fenrir.

p.58. *Milosz.* Specifically *A Song on the End of the World,* from 1944.

Acknowledgements

'Pigeon' won the Cannon Poets Sonnet or Not Poetry Prize 2013 and was published in *The Cannon's Mouth*.

'Arvandil's toe' came second in the Troubadour Poetry Prize 2014, and was published online. 'Hare' was a commended poem in the previous year's competition.

'Loki as falcon' came second in the Sentinel Poetry Competition 2016, and 'In your hands' was highly commended in the same competition. Both were published in *Sentinel Literary Quarterly*.

'Ash' was commended in the Ware Poets Open Poetry Competition 2013 and published in their competition pamphlet.

'Idun' was commended in the McLellan Poetry Competition 2016 and published online.

'Swan' was a runner up in the Welsh Poetry Competition 2015 and was published online, and subsequently in *Ten Years On*, a competition anthology.

Other poems, or earlier versions, were published in the *New Welsh Review, Orbis, The Frogmore Papers, Ink Sweat & Tears, Eye Flash Poetry* and *Dear World* (a Cheltenham Poetry Festival Pamphlet).

A number of these poems were broadcast on Swindon 105.5's 'Art2Art' programme, and I would like to thank the presenter, Kim Wright, for arranging this.

I would also like to thank Amy Wack, Alistair Noon, Carolyne Larrington and Suzanne Cawsey for valuable comments on earlier drafts, as well as Anna Saunders, Angela France, Christine Whittemore, Alwyn Marriage, Helen Ivory, Alison Brackenbury, Kate North, Maggie Butt and Adam Wyeth, as well as all at Seren, for support and encouragement over the years.